D1607020

SPOTLIGHT ON SOCIAL AND EMOTIONAL LEARNING

CONNECTING WITH OTHERS

SOCIAL ENGAGEMENT

JENNIFER LOMBARDO

PowerKiDS
press™

NEW YORK

Published in 2020 by The Rosen Publishing Group, Inc.
29 East 21st Street, New York, NY 10010

Editor: Elizabeth Krajnik
Cover Design: Michael Flynn

Photo Credits: Cover gradyreese/E+/Getty Images; cover, pp. 1, 3–4, 6–8, 10, 12–18; 20, 22–24 (background) TairA/Shutterstock.com; p. 5 Rawpixel.com/Shutterstock.com; p. 6 Africa Studio/Shutterstock.com; p. 7 hedgehog94/Shutterstock.com; pp. 8, 17 Hero Images/Getty Images; p. 9 mirjana ristic damjanovic/Shutterstock.com; p. 11 SOPA Images/LightRocket/Getty Images; p. 12 Nancy Honey/Cultura/Getty Images; p. 13 Image Source/DigitalVision/Getty Images; pp. 14, 15 Camille Tokerud/The Image Bank/Getty Images; p. 16 Hindustan Times/Getty Images; p. 19 Nigel Waldron/Getty Images Entertainment/Getty Images; p. 21 Hill Street Studios LLC/DigitalVision/Getty Images; p. 22 barbsimages/Shutterstock.com.

Cataloging-in-Publication Data

Names: Lombardo, Jennifer.
Title: Connecting with others: social engagement / Jennifer Lombardo.
Description: New York : PowerKids Press, 2020. | Series: Spotlight on social and emotional learning | Includes glossary and index.
Identifiers: ISBN 9781725306592 (pbk.) | ISBN 9781725306622 (library bound) | ISBN 9781725306608 (6pack)
Subjects: LCSH: Social action--Juvenile literature. | Social advocacy--Juvenile literature. | Voluntarism--Juvenile literature. | Social participation--Juvenile literature. | Political participation--Juvenile literature.
Classification: LCC HN18.3 L6575 2020 | DDC 361.2--dc23

Manufactured in the United States of America

CPSIA Compliance Information: Batch #CWPK20. For further information contact Rosen Publishing, New York, New York at 1-800-237-9932.

CONTENTS

CHAPTER ONE

WHAT IS SOCIAL ENGAGEMENT?

When people work together to make their communities better, it's called social engagement. Sometimes it's also called social **participation** or social **involvement**. Getting involved in your community can take many different forms, including **donating** things such as clothes or food to people or groups that need them, **volunteering**, or joining a club.

Getting involved in your community is easier than you might think. Have you ever collected canned food to donate to a food bank? Have you done a service project with a group, such as a Girl or Boy Scout troop? Have you made posters to help people learn about a cause you feel strongly about? Do you go somewhere, such as a church, to practice your religion every week? Do you take care of a community garden? If you said yes to any of these, then you've participated in your community!

Planting trees to make a neighborhood look nicer is one way people can have an impact, or effect, on their community.

CHAPTER TWO

WHY IS SOCIAL ENGAGEMENT IMPORTANT?

There are many benefits to social engagement. It gives people something fun and rewarding to do, which can make them happy. At volunteer events, people can make new friends who are different from them and the people they already know. Having a **diverse** friend group is important because it can help people learn new things. You might learn about a different **culture**, or you might become friends with someone older than you who can give you good advice.

Making friends from different backgrounds can help you look at the world from a new point of view.

Working together with a diverse group can teach people new things that will help them for the rest of their lives. For example, when people work as a group, sometimes they disagree. This is called conflict. Social engagement helps teach people how to talk about problems and solve conflicts without fighting.

Social engagement isn't just good for **individuals**. It's also good for the community. When the community gets better, everyone wins. One simple action could have more than one benefit. For example, someone who has more food than they need can donate some of it to a food bank. This helps people who don't have enough food. When kids have enough to eat, they often get better grades in school.

You don't need to have a lot of money to participate in your community. People can donate their time instead of money or things. You might decide that, instead of spending a Saturday reading or playing video games, you want to talk to people in a nursing home who don't get many visitors. This will make the people you're visiting very happy, and you might make a new friend!

People living in nursing homes may have many stories to tell you. These stories might help you learn something new about how other people live.

CHAPTER THREE

DIFFERENT WAYS TO HELP

There are three major types of service-related social engagement: direct service, indirect service, and advocacy. Direct service is when a person donates their time to work directly with other people. One example of direct service is volunteering with a **tutoring** program to help other students learn a subject they have trouble with. Indirect service is when someone donates or collects money for a cause or things other people might need or want. This could include food, clothing, or toys at Christmas.

Advocacy means making people aware of issues they can help change. For example, if you're interested in keeping you and your friends healthy, you can support organizations such as Truth, which tells people facts about cigarettes through TV and billboard ads to **encourage** people not to smoke.

Helping organize an event or march for a cause you believe in, such as women's rights, is one form of advocacy.

EQUALITY

SOLIDARITY WITH WOMENS STRUGGLES ALL OVER THE WORLD

VIOLNE AGINST WMN

CHAPTER FOUR

CAN SOCIAL ENGAGEMENT BE BAD?

Social engagement is usually a good thing, but sometimes it can cause problems for people. If someone starts taking part in a group that encourages its members to do bad things, such as **vandalizing** buildings or stealing things, it's not helping the community. Sometimes people feel like joining a gang will be fun and exciting, but they may get arrested or badly hurt. They're often hurting others in their community.

If you take on too much volunteer work, you may not have enough time to study, and your grades may be affected.

Social engagement can also cause problems if someone tries to do too much. Some people like volunteering so much that they say yes to everything they're asked to do. If someone does so many things in their community that they never have time to relax or see their family and friends, they may become **stressed**, which is bad for a person's health.

CHAPTER FIVE

HOW TO GET INVOLVED

There are so many different ways people can participate in their community that they may not know where to start. This makes it hard for people to choose what they'd like to do. Breaking the list of things down into smaller parts can help you decide.

Volunteering can be fun if you pick something you like to do.

The first thing to think about is what you like. Do you like animals? You might like to volunteer at an animal shelter. Do you like hearing your grandparents' stories about when they were young? You may like to visit people in a nursing home. Do you like to learn new things? You can choose something you've never done before and learn a new skill. People who want to get involved often look online to see which places in their community are looking for volunteers.

Making posters is a good way to spread the word about something you feel strongly about.

The second thing to think about is how much time you have. Many students have things to do after school, such as homework and chores, so they may not have a lot of time to volunteer. If you feel strongly about a cause but don't have time to go to group meetings, you can create your own advocacy project, such as putting up posters or making a website. You can also work on an indirect service project, such as saving your money to buy something to donate to a homeless shelter.

Joining a club or going to a religious service is also a good way to get involved in your community when you don't have a lot of spare time. These types of organizations may help people make new friends, learn how to work together, and make good decisions.

CHAPTER SIX

BIG OR SMALL

Sometimes social engagement directly affects only a small group of people, such as the people in one school or one town. However, this doesn't mean small actions aren't important. Small actions can still help people. Other times, your actions can affect a lot of people at once. They may even change the world!

Malala Yousafzai, a young Pakistani woman, became famous for speaking out against the Taliban, a **terrorist** organization. The Taliban banned girls from going to school, but Malala believes everyone should be able to get an education. She created her own organization to help girls around the world go to school. Even after the Taliban tried to kill Malala and injured her, she kept working toward her goal. Not everyone can do something like this, but that doesn't mean you can't try to create positive change.

In 2014, when Malala Yousafzai was just 17 years old, she won the Nobel Peace Prize for her social engagement work.

CHAPTER SEVEN

FINDING OPPORTUNITIES

Most schools have student clubs that meet after school or on weekends. For example, someone who likes to draw might join an art club. These clubs can help people meet new people and make new friends they might never have met otherwise.

Sometimes a person doesn't want to join any of the clubs their school offers, but this doesn't mean there's nothing they can do. People can use the Internet to find places that are looking for volunteers or clubs that aren't run by a school. If someone can't find anything they're interested in, they can make their own club and invite other people to join. Another way to get involved is for people to ask their friends what kinds of clubs they're involved in. Many people join clubs after being invited to a meeting by a friend.

Taking part in a community garden is a great way to get involved. You'll probably make some new friends and learn something new.

CHAPTER EIGHT

PICKING A CLUB

Different types of clubs have different goals. Some are just for fun or to help people get better at something. For example, some clubs help people become better writers. The members of these clubs give each other advice and encouragement. Other clubs exist only to help their members find volunteer opportunities. Volunteering with others can be a great way to make friends.

Some clubs combine fun and volunteering. For example, Girl Scouts and Boy Scouts do things such as make crafts and go camping, but they also work together on service projects. Sometimes they combine fun and service at the same time by doing something like making blankets to donate to a nursing home or homeless shelter. If you have enough spare time, you could join two or three different types of groups!

GLOSSARY

culture (KUHL-chuhr) The beliefs and ways of life of a certain group of people.

diverse (DY-vers) Different or varied.

donate (DOH-nayt) To give something in order to help a person or organization.

encourage (ihn-KUHR-ihj) To try to win over to a cause or action.

individual (in-duh-VIHJ-wuhl) A single member of a group.

involvement (ihn-VAHLV-muhnt) The state, act, or fact of being involved, or taking part in something.

participation (pahr-tih-suh-PAY-shuhn) The act of taking part in something.

stressed (STREHST) Feeling very worried or anxious.

terrorist (TEHR-uhr-ist) Having to do with using violence and fear to achieve a goal.

tutor (TOO-tuhr) To provide someone with private instruction.

vandalize (VAN-duh-lyze) To destroy or damage property on purpose.

volunteer (vah-luhn-TEER) To do something to help because you want to do it.

INDEX

PRIMARY SOURCE LIST

Page 11
Kids hold placards as they take part in a women's rights protest. Photograph. Nikolas Joao Kokovlis. November 24, 2018. SOPA Images and LightRocket via Getty Images.

Page 16
Children Participate in Parsi Summer Camp in Mumbai. Photograph. Pratham Gokhale. May 19, 2015. *Hindustan Times* via Getty Images.

Page 19
Malala Yousafzai. Photograph. Michael Gottschalk. February 4, 2016. Photothek via Getty Images.

WEBSITES

Due to the changing nature of Internet links, PowerKids Press has developed an online list of websites related to the subject of this book. This site is updated regularly. Please use this link to access the list: www.powerkidslinks.com/SSEL/engagement